Published 2017

Bright Tomorrow Books

ISBN-13: 978-1544982779

ISBN-10: 1544982771

Tin Baths And Coal Fires

Ethel Oates

This book is dedicated to

my grandchildren Mali, Lloyd and Elis.

And also to

Lynda, my patient teacher, and my fellow scribes

who encouraged me to write.

Contents

Play Paradise

Much has been written about Senghenydd the village of my childhood. There had been a huge colliery disaster in October 1913 and four hundred and thirty nine men were killed. Senghenydd in the past had been called 'The Valley of Tears', but I can only think of it as the sweetest place. Some of the long and short terraced streets are built quite high on the sides of the valley. Many have known three or four generations of the same families. Some have housed large families who have shared poverty, grief, love, and joy. Time cannot obliterate the strong character of these houses or dim the memories, good and bad, of those who have lived in them.

Although it was forbidden, many of the children in our street and the surrounding terraces played in and around the ruins of the old Universal Colliery. Our parent's warnings that it was dangerous fell on deaf ears. The washeries where the coal had been washed were situated very close to Parc Terrace where I lived. They were low sloping structures, about half a dozen of them. Sometimes we were content just to sit on them and make daisy chains, chanting nursery rhymes or singing songs, our mothers glancing at us whilst shaking mats or scouring doorsteps. About a quarter of a mile beyond where the streets ended, were the two cream brick giant chimney stacks of the colliery. We would run around the base platforms on which they were built. There was very little room on the ledge and we shrieked and laughed when we teetered dangerously close to the edge. The platforms had a forty or fifty foot drop. We were always giddy when we stared upwards. The cream bricks seemed to touch the white clouds and our small arms stretched out and hugged the chimneys to keep us steady.

A mile beyond the chimney stacks stood our play paradise – the shell of a large red brick building called The Compressor. It had once housed the pump for fresh air to go down underground to the colliery. It was three storeys high with large areas of the grey roof slates missing. Inside were masses of large jagged concrete slabs with twisted rusted wire running through them; like giant icebergs all at strange and weird angles. Small groups of nettles grew randomly, and clumps of weeds grew out of its skeleton walls. The Comp, as we affectionately called it, was a truly dangerous place to play. It had an unpleasant dank smell. Sheep sometimes wandered in so there were droppings everywhere. The sheep always ran away when they heard us approaching. It was our private playground. We could scream and shout and sing as loudly as we liked. In all its ugliness we loved it. Like a motionless, voiceless Svengali, this old ruin of a building attracted us like a magnet.

A watchman called Mr Carriegar lived very near and his barking dogs always alerted us that he was coming. We were usually a group of seven or eight boys and girls: Tony Williams, Georgie White, Bertie Griffiths, Gerald Meredith, June Thomas, Sylvia Meredith, my cousins Hilary and Madeleine Davies, and my sister and I, Joyce and Ethel James. Like all the other girls I could only climb to the second level of The Comp. The boys, however, could climb easily to the highest parts, their Tarzan shrieks echoing around this huge semi-structure. Bertie Griffiths, in his plimsolls, was so fleet of foot, he could scale a sheer wall in seconds. We would gaze in awe, dazzled by the brilliance of his agility and lack of fear. It was as if he were a famous circus performer. Sometimes the boys would encourage us girls to climb higher, pulling us up, stretching limbs until they hurt. We loved it, never caring that our knees were scratched almost raw on the concrete.

It was a fascination to be inside a building yet seemingly outside with the sky visible through gaps of wall, roof, and missing floor. There was nothing lovely in this place only the sound of our laughter. I would look up and watch clouds pass by on a blue summer sky. When it rained we would skip around gaping black chasms of darkness in the floors, to shelter underneath an intact piece of roof. The boys would leap over these gaping holes with no fear. We knew we should run home to the dry safety of our homes but were blissfully happy, and unaware in a way that only young children can be, of the awful grief we might have caused. I can still smell the colourless glycerine and rosewater that was used to sooth chapped hands and knees. In a small plain white bottle, at two shillings it was an extravagant buy for my mother. My three sisters and I shared the small bottle and it had to last a whole week. Early evening when the zinc bath, which hung on a nail in the backyard wall, was brought in and we were bathed, my mother would gently pat the lotion on our knees and the backs of our hands. 'Ouch ouch' we would shout in turn, though I still longed for a bottle all to myself it smelled so lovely. Our lovely long wyncette nighties were soft on our scraped legs.

My childhood friends are scattered now, though occasionally I see Bertie, his feet now encased in smart leather shoes, he semi-shuffles to the tune of old age and I wonder if he longs to step back in time for a day, as I do.

My Bedroom

In the bedroom there was little space to move around. I always shared with three of my sisters who were all younger than me. Next to me in age was my sister Joyce – we looked similar as we both had dark plaited hair – then came Ray, a blue eyed blonde. Ray was a happy child always sitting on my mother's knee and kissing her. Linda, the youngest, was small with fine hair. Linda had to wear glasses from the age of twenty-two months, they were little round wire glasses; she was so pretty and cute – the runt of the litter my mother would say.

Our bedroom was at the back of the house and over-looked our small backyard. Behind the stone garden wall was Grove Terrace and behind that some trees were visible, part of a small wood. When I gazed at them through the rattling sash window at bedtime their dark silhouettes swayed against the night sky and always frightened me. The window was low and a bamboo rod, suspended on two nails, held a piece of net curtain half way up. Larger plain green, dyed cotton curtains were on a wooden pole. They were hard to tug closed. At seven-thirty each night we would climb the stairs with a chorus of, 'Goodnight, God bless.' We would wee in turn into the chamber pot. Our Joyce always said the same thing, 'Let me go first.'

A large metal, coiled spring, bed took up most of the room. The top and bottom end had black round slated rods and the thicker corner posts had brass bulbous parts on top of them that moved around, loosened over the years by small fingers constantly twisting them. When one of us turned or moved in restless slumber the springs squeaked and the bed swayed as if in distress. It always seemed to me the bed was seldom ever still. Its mattress was back and white striped and flock filled (a material that was like shredded wool) and the long bolster pillow was also flock filled .Our bed sheets were always winceyette soft and warm. Our bedcover, which had been made by my father's mother on her treadle sewing machine, was patchwork, padded and thick. For endless hours my younger sister and I would scrutinize the various pieces of multi coloured floral fabric, taking turns to choose a square each. It was a silly pointless game that we loved.

On the wall opposite the bed was a tiny metal fire grate painted pink. A fire was only lit if someone was ill. Next to the grate stood a large black gloomy wardrobe with one bottom drawer and metal drop handles. Laid out on the dressing table was a glass trinket set on crocheted silk circular mats that my aunt had made. I thought the cheap thick and clumsy white glass trinket set to be one of the loveliest things in our house. I was forever lifting the lids of the two little bowls, cupping and even caressing the matching candlesticks in my hands. A flat small tray and a ring dish completed the set.

Our bedroom wallpaper had small clusters of rosebuds with a border of deeper pink larger roses that was pasted directly underneath the ceiling, it drew attention to the ugly black cracks that reminded me of lightning flashes. I hated them. Bright pink and grey lino covered the wooden floorboards. It was as cold as marble underneath slipper-less feet. At the side of the bed was a small paisley-patterned rug and underneath the bed was the plain white china chamber pot. My mother forever warned us not to spill the pot on the rug, as she considered this rug a small piece of luxury.

The skirting boards of the room were about six inches high and it was a very big drawback that there were large gaps of some two inches in places at the bottom of it. If a button, hair slide or coin were dropped it would disappear under the gaps. My mother had bought me a small silver cross for my seventh birthday and it was lost for five years underneath the skirting. I was thrilled when she retrieved it one day when cleaning. I still have it.

I was known to be the most nervous of our family and I remember my mother bringing me into her bed when I awoke from nightmares. The oil lamp she had in her room cast huge shadows on the wall and did nothing to comfort me.

There were no toys in our room. Our main family game, which was kept downstairs, was a dilapidated box that contained a cardboard Ludo board with the game Snakes and Ladders on the reverse side.

In spite of the cold cramped space of the bedroom, I remember with fondness how warm we were in bed, cuddled up to one another under patched flannel blankets that my mother had repaired countless times. Whispering, singing, sharing childish secrets before we fell asleep in the crowded bed.

Cousin Billy

One winter's day in December, my sisters and I ran home from school. There was a magical excitement in the air that children can feel when they see the first Christmas trees appearing in parlour windows. Our cousin Billy who lived in Grove Terrace was just turning the street corner. He waved to us. Hiya we chorused, proud to show our friends that he was related to us. Billy was an amateur boxer and very popular in the village. People said he was an excellent dancer too. That seemed strange to me. I couldn't imagine him dancing. Such a tall, broad, gentle giant of a man. He was about thirty-years-old. I was only ten. Billy had four children two boys and two girls all younger than me.

We were all hungry and when we opened the front door the appetising smell of simmering broth with leeks and parsley wafted down the passageway. My older sister was helping my mother get the tea ready and was lifting teisen lap from the oven. The smells impregnated the house. There was a welcoming coal fire in the gleaming black leaded grate that was my mother's pride and joy, though it took an hour to clean every morning. On occasions when I wasn't well enough to attend school and the daily ritual of the fire grate cleaning began, I would be allowed to curl up on the cushioned rocking chair at the side of the grate and watch. First my mother spread sheets of newspapers out to avoid getting the cheap coconut matting dirty. The half dozen candlesticks were lifted down from the mantle shelf to be cleaned with liquid Brasso; they graduated in size and gleamed like gold. The mantle shelf had a decorative brass patterned edging tacked onto it and below this a brass rod was suspended, all cleaned and polished with Brasso.

On the hobs of the grate a large black leaded kettle simmered and sung all day. Resting on the fender was a blower. It was a large sheet of metal resembling a shield. This was placed on top of the fire to rest against the chimney breast. The blower caused the fire to draw in air. Like an angry lion, the flames roared behind it.

Sometimes late in the evening, socks would be draped over the brass rod to air, but never in daytime. The fireplace seemed majestic to me such was my mother's devotion in keeping it shining and bright. Black lead and Brasso competed for attention. She would have small beads of perspiration all over her face after cleaning it. The blackened rags and stained brushes were put away in a cardboard box. Everyone admired the grate but I secretly resented the fact my mother seemed to be its slave.

I remember December 19th. My sisters and I came downstairs in our winceyette nightgowns. Breakfast toast was keeping warm on the fender. It seemed a day like any other. The wind was howling and rattling our back kitchen sash window like an invisible, uninvited, guest trying to get in. When we were dressed and ready, black fur pixie hats were fastened securely under our chins before we set off up the rough hill at the side of Stanley Street to school. The hats had been made out of an old simulated fur coat that had belonged to a neighbour. When we walked home from school at tea time the first of winter's snow-flakes covered our hats, swirling around us, kissing our noses and landing on eye lashes like soft feathers. We shrieked with delight.

I knew something was wrong when I came into the house. The fire burned brightly banked high with small coal, but the grate was not cleaned. It was thick with last night's coal dust . 'Hurry up and eat your tea quickly girls,' my mother said. 'I want you in bed early tonight.' Her eyes were red as if they had been rubbed. 'You've been crying, our Mam,' I accused.

My father and brothers were out the back kitchen. The door was closed as they bathed in a tin bath by a smaller fire grate. Their voices were whispering but I heard my uncle Dai's name mentioned once or twice. My father, older brothers cous-ins and uncles were all coalminers and worked at 'The Windsor Colliery' in Abertridwr. After we had eaten our tea, my mother told us quite simply that cousin Billy had been killed at his job underground at the mine.

Billy's funeral was held on Christmas Eve.

Street Games

Skipping with a piece of coconut rope was a favourite game for the girls, although the constant twirling of the rope and it's constant beating on stone caused it to break numerous times, it was re knotted and the game continued. Two girls could skip together, one jumping into the twirling rope after the other had made room for her to jump in. We would chant songs while skipping: 'Cobbler, cobbler, mend my shoes, get them done by half past two...'and 'Eber Kenezer king of the Jews bought his wife a pair of shoes. When the shoes began to wear Eber Kenezer began to swear.'

There was very little traffic, so we performed 'The Farmer's In His Den' in the middle of the road in a circle, holding hands. We sang, 'The farmer wants a wife.' and the chosen farmer in the centre, selected a wife to join him and so on. The chase game called Touch or Tag, wore us out by bedtime.

You might be lucky enough to have a wooden spinning top and wooden whip with string threaded through. We would search for old sweet wrappers and stick small coloured pieces on top, moving the coloured paper, changing the position, fascinated by the spinning circles. They looked so pretty and almost hypnotised us as they spun. 'Come and see mine,' I would call to my sisters and friends.

Hopscotch was a great game we loved. We scratched six

numbers with a small stone onto the square pavement slabs. On one foot we skipped another small stone around. There was a circle version of this game. Our shoes were scuffed playing this game to my mother's dismay she always polished our shoes every evening. The boys huddled in small groups on the pavement playing with glass marbles.

Sometimes someone would be lucky enough to find a discarded bike wheel. A father or older brother would remove the spokes from the wheel, and with a piece of metal bent into a hook shape, the lucky boy would race around controlling and guiding the wheel with the hook. The boys called them Bowlies. No one minded running an errand if you had a Bowlie to run with. Another great thing for the boys was when an old pram was being thrown out. The four wheels would be made into what they called a gambo. The wheels were transformed into a gambo by fixing a piece of wood across it to sit on, then a piece of rope tied each side of the front to steer it, no brake other than an extended foot held sharply down. Fathers would often tack some hobnails or segs as they were sometimes called into the bottom of shoes to make them last longer. Two maybe three children would ride on the crudely-made fabulous gambo as it careered down the slopes at the side of the streets.

Near the railway station, a small piece of railway line, that belonged to the colliery had been left. On this small piece of railway line, were the skeletal remains of an old coal dram. It could be pushed and moved only a short distance, as earth and weeds had swallowed the small piece of track that it stood on. The wheels were so heavy and thick it took three or four of us to move it. One day a small group of us were struggling to push the dram, Joyce's leg was on the track, we stopped as Joyce toppled to the side. The sharp edge of the wheel had knocked her shin. Joyce fell to the side. We all gathered around her, there was a nasty cut and blood ran down her leg soaking into her white ankle sock.' Go get our dad quickly' I shouted to my sister Ray. Our father came running down the grassy bank with an anxious look on his face. He carried Joyce up to our house, it was directly in front of the Railway Station. My father put Joyce down on the settee, while my worried mother fussed putting cushions behind her. We all crowded in to watch the drama, my mother ushered us all outside, while the Doctor was sent for. Joyce needed a few stitches in her wound, my mother ran to the outside toilet at the back of our garden and shut herself in until the procedure was over. For days she was cosseted and allowed to sit in my fathers' rocking chair with cushions and a blanket.

Many hours were spent below the grass bank that the terraced street was built on. Each of us would gather stones and form a square with them to play 'house'. There were tips on the grassy bank opposite the houses where people threw their coal ashes and other refuse. Some years later the council would send a lorry around to collect the ashes that were left in old zinc buckets at the kerb. On the tips we would find old jam jars that we'd wash in the small stream nearby and fill with wild flowers. They were placed on a large stone that was our pretend table. Old shoe polish tins found on the tip were filled with a mixture of dirt with water and buttercups and daisy heads were pressed gently on top to complete our mud pies. Playing mud pies gave hours of joy. Of course you had the task of fashioning an oven out of old bricks and stones, to bake them in.

We washed our muddy hands in the cold water of the stream. 'Oh it's freezing,' I shouted to the others. 'Look at the mud splashes on your dress.'

'You will have a row of our Mam,' my sisters warned.

Glorious cloudless days, of contentment and fun when the world had barely touched us.

Childhood Days

I remember whipping wooden tops
with sweet papers spinning, stuck on top.
Hop scotch, sliding stones, scuffed shoes.
Children skipping, holding hands, jumping in twos.
Earth mixed with water and mud pies were made.
Daisy chains on small heads were laid.
Long rambles to a crystal clear spring.
Sweet are the memories of these happy things.

My Mother

My aunt Elsie was my father's sister. She and my uncle Griff had two daughters, my cousins Madeline and Hilary. As a child I was in awe of my aunt. I thought she was as glamorous as any film star. My sister and I would sit on the kerbside outside her house and a few times a week she would come out dressed immaculately.

My aunt wore the highest heeled shoes. One pair I particular loved: they were white with a bow on the front of them. Her hennaed hair she wore in little curls piled high on her head. Most of all I loved the scarlet lipstick that she was never without. I promised myself that when I grew up, I would wear exactly the same shade.

In stark contrast to my aunt, my mother was a strictly no nonsense woman. Never the merest touch of make-up of any kind. You can't beat soap and water for the skin, was her motto. High heels were out of the question as she suffered with varicose veins, bunions and corns. She had never owned a pair of high heeled shoes, or had any desire to. The only night out my mother had was when attending the sisterhood meeting in the chapel that we went to. How boring I used to think in my small child's mind. You could tell my mother's hair had once been black but it had more grey than black in the early fifties. It was worn in a style that was quick and simple to do. Parted in the middle it would be combed down an old piece of material tied around her head in a band then the hair rolled around the band. There was an alarming story my mother told us about a time when bobbed hair became fashionable for women. Most women were taking to this easy popular style. Of course, my mother could not afford to go to a salon so a lady who lived in the street behind, and obviously fancied herself as a hairdresser as a means to making a few shillings, cut my mother's very long lovely hair. My mother hadn't consulted my father about this decision and when he got home from work he flew into an uncontrollable rage and started smashing dishes that were on the Welsh dresser, some of which had been wedding presents. My mother sent my brother to go and fetch my father's mother who lived in Grove Terrace the street behind us. She came down to the house right away and gave him a telling off. The poor woman who had cut my mother's hair, on hearing the row and the smashing of china, had run and locked herself in her house. When reminded of his tantrum that day he would say women who had short hair were too lazy to look after it. There was no reasoning with him about hair.

There was a rigid routine in our house. We were all washed by six thirty and in our nightdresses our plaited hair un-done and combed out. Our school clothes neatly folded, a piece of toast for supper, then tucked in bed by seven. My mother would kiss us goodnight and close the bedroom window trying to shut out the sounds of other children playing in the street. The old wooden sash windows did nothing to block out the shrieks, and the chanting of skipping rhymes that we could still hear. Countless times I wished we could have stayed up later. However within minutes we would all be asleep.

Our breakfast was always ready for us when we came downstairs in the morning. School gymslips were pressed, the pleats sewn with large tacking stitches beforehand. My mother would have been up hours earlier to make breakfast for my father and older brothers before they went to work. I sometimes wondered if she stayed up all night.

It was only as an adult, and in my mother's final years, when I bathed her small worn fragile body could I see how truly beautiful she was. Her legs were covered from top to bottom in varicose veins through too many years of child bearing. Her hair, which had once been glossy and black, had now turned to silver. She reached her hands out to me and I gently took them, the fingers bent with arthritis and knuckles enlarged through years of rubbing clothes on a scrubbing board; I marvelled at how breathtakingly lovely they were. I gently dried and combed her hair as if she was now the child and wondered how I could have not seen my mother's beauty sooner.

School Days

Senghenydd Infant and Junior schools and the Boys' school were on the side of the valley behind the last rows of terraced streets. Parc Terrace, where my family lived, was on the opposite side of the valley. Our walk to school was hard and it was hard also for the children of Grove Terrace, Station Terrace and the children who lived at the top of the valley in the four terraced streets. Our walk to school meant you had to climb a rugged hill of stones that was at the side of Stanley Street. It was a tough walk on a dry day, on winter wet and windy days even worse with our feet slip -sliding on the huge stones. Our polished shoes were muddy and soggy before the school day had even properly began.

On the corner of the main road, before you reached Stanley Street, was Mr Brown's shop. On one side of the store he sold fruit and vegetables, bottles of Tizer, lemonade, dandelion and burdock and American cream soda. On the other side of the store he sold biscuits, flour and various dry products. The counter displayed rows of glass sweet jars that contained mostly boiled sweets: pear drops, sherbet lemons, fruit drops, glass mints, and twisted barley sugar. Because I gazed at the jars so often I also remember wine gums, dolly mixtures, liquorice torpedoes, and marzipan tea cakes. Once a week on a Saturday we were allowed to choose two ounces of sweets each, served in a little triangle shaped paper bag. My mother allowed us to stay up later since there was no school the next day and while eating our sweets we would all listen to the Saturday night theatre play on the wireless.

On school days we only had a penny to spend and into Mr Brown's shop we would go. Our favourite choice for a penny was a stick of Spanish root from a jar on the counter. We sucked and chewed these little sticks of wood until they were shredded and all the flavour gone. The juice was swallowed and our spittle and mouths turned yellow. The funny thing was, I couldn't make up my mind if I really liked it or not. Now the idea of it makes me feel sick.

Mr Brown was elderly and not exactly jovial. He was, however, a very shrewd business man and would sell us his damaged apples for a penny, using a small knife to cut out the damaged part.

The school bell would ring and we would form orderly class lines to go in. First there was always a school assembly in the large hall that was used for sport and school concerts. Our head mistress conducted the assembly with the music teacher accompanying the hymn singing on a very ancient piano. The Lord's Prayer was always recited and sometimes there were special announcements. I disliked most of my school lessons, only favouring a few: Art, essay writing, and Cookery.

One of my happiest times was when we had netball practise. The school yard was marked out as a court and the two heavy wooden netball posts were carried outside and the game would begin. If you were not in a team you were a spectator and booed or cheered accordingly. The games were always a lot of fun. Sports day for the school was sometimes held over on

Senghenydd Rec where the local rugby team played.

If you had school dinners as my sisters and I did, the teachers in turn escorted us in an orderly line down to The Square, where adjacent to The Gwryn Milwr Hotel, there were some upstairs rooms where the dinners were served on tables of ten or twelve. Heads bowed, there would be a short prayer and two girls would be selected to pass the plates, cutlery, and desert dishes around the table. We were allowed to talk so the chatter and noise was very loud. After dinner we were allowed to make our own journey back up to the school unchaperoned.

I

II

III

IV

V

VI

VII

VIII

The Rec

At the top of the village, cut out of the turf at the base of one of the mountains, there is a large flat area a hundred or more yards square. Its banks overlook the village. This is the old rugby pitch constructed by the Universal Colliery in 1910. In my childhood the Senghenydd Rugby team played matches on it. In previous years it had been fenced. In the summer, my sisters and I would go to the Rec, take a packed lunch consisting of jam sandwiches and maybe a piece of teisen lap my mother had made. We'd perch on the corner-most edge legs hanging over its banks as though on some giant slab of cake. The view of the village was wonderful. You could not hear any of the sounds of village life, car engines, church bells or the noisy belching steam train that came up from Cardiff to the end of the line railway station. Grey slates on rooftops shone like silver in the glare of the bright summer sun. Tarmac roads glistened like marcasite. Smoke lazily twirled out of chimneys and window panes winked in the setting sun. Butterflies danced a slow summer waltz over foxgloves and ferns on the slopes below.

The Rec was not only used for rugby. Whitsun church teas, school sports day, fetes and carnivals it also drew village people together. Children playing hopscotch or skipping would suddenly become as still as statues, ears listening intently. When the local jazz band came into view, excitement filled the air. It was as much a treat as a bar of chocolate. The band would march from Abertridwr, through Senghenydd and straight up to the Rec. Children followed like the rats in 'The Pied Piper of Hamelin'. Around and around the Rec they'd march then back down into the village again. The drum banged loudly, and the sound from the kazoos the girls played was magic floating in the air and it made everyone feel so happy.

In August 1919 there was a ceremony when villagers honoured their war heroes. Thousands of people came to see a Colonel present military medals with, of course, a male voice choir present and the Silver Colliery Band.

In the evening courting couples sat on the edge of the Rec with arms encircling waists. Only the gurgling stream, the crickets song or the bleating of a sheep would distract them from their hopes and dreams. The excitement of rugby, the laughter of carnivals, the joy of jazz bands and the pride of heroes are some of the emotions that still hang like a magical canopy over this chunk of flattened turf that was once the centrepiece for community life.

Senghenydd Rec

Above the valley of my birth
a shelf cut out of weed filled earth.
Segments of my childhood years
spent on emerald flattened turf
shaped so many years ago
I turn the key in memories door.

My eye a shuttered camera lens
upon my cheek a tear descends.
Distant windows give knowing winks
emotions sweep me as I blink.
Gathered crowds, a mighty roar
cheering loud a great try just scored.

Clapping clink of Whitsun teas
marching music, Jazz bands please.
Heartache, war years, painfully pass
heroes welcomed home at last.
Honoured here on this mountainside
when hearts were swollen, filled with pride.

Towser

Our family pet was a dog called Towser. My older brothers had named him. My father brought him home one day and he was not exactly a puppy but he was young. I never knew where he originated from and didn't care. My three younger sisters and I loved him so much, as did the older siblings in our family who were all working. Towser followed us younger ones around wherever we went. He had a collar but no lead, it wasn't needed. Towser's coat was the colour of yellow sand, he had a white patch above his nose. His chest and paws were also white. Towser was not tall but had a massive chest. With four of us continually patting and stroking him, he loved us as much as we unconditionally loved him.

Other dogs in adjacent streets always barked at Towser, spoiling for a fight. However, he always obeyed us – though sometimes reluctantly. 'Come on boy!' we would urge him home and he always followed us. One dog in particular was always snarling and yapping at him. We lived in number five and this dog belonged to my two cousins Madeleine and Hilary who lived in number eighteen. His name was Smudge and was certainly no match for Towser. I hated to admit it because I hated his constant challenging barking to Towser, but Smudge was a pretty dog, pale golden blonde in colour with a long curly tail. He was the yappyiest dog I had ever heard. He simply could not set eyes on Towser without going into a barking frenzy. Barking mad, I thought, desperate for a fight, when I was sure it was obvious to everyone Towser could tear him to pieces. Smudge always circled Towser, barking insanely; Towser barked back but never went near him as he always listened to us when we called him. These confrontations distressed us immensely.

We always had to pass my cousin's house when we returned from rambles up the mountain. Or days when we would spend hours sliding down the banks of The Rec rugby pitch on pieces of cardboard. Or maybe returning from another beauty spot we called The Water Quarry. We related these traumatic barking bouts to our father; sad to say, I felt my father wished Towser would retaliate to Smudge and teach him a lesson, though he never said so. He said we had spoilt Towser from being a real dog! Whatever could he mean? Those words were lost on us.

One day we were playing right outside our house when Smudge suddenly appeared, snarling and barking as usual. I couldn't understand it. There was no bone to quarrel over so why couldn't the dogs be friends? The barking grew so loud and when Smudge got close enough to Towser he bit one of his hind legs. Towser spun around and in a split second locked jaws with Smudge. The awful barking stopped and a terrible growling noise came from deep within the two dogs. It was a hateful awful sound. Someone came out of their house with a bowl of cold water and threw it over the dogs. They didn't move, not one inch. Towser finally had hold of his tormentor and wouldn't obey us. I just couldn't believe it. The awful scene filled me with horror but I could not tear myself to look away. My brother, Alan, had hold of Towser's rear end and another man had hold of Smudge. Where was my father? I wondered. I could not understand why he was not with my brother. I thought my heart would break. A crowd had gathered to see the spectacle of two animals with locked jaws. I fought to keep my tears back. At last my father came out of our house, to my horror holding the iron poker that was always kept on the side of our fire grate. To my relief he ran his hand up and down it to show all it was cold. He had been cooling it in a bucket of water, hence his delay in coming out. It only took a second for my dad to prise the jaws apart.

Towser was taken indoors and Smudge carried home. I don't think either dog had a mark on them. I'm sure it all happened in a few minutes but to my sisters and I it seemed like an eternity and is etched in my memory forever. The crowd quickly dispersed. It would be nice to say Smudge quietened down after that, but he never did.

Outings

As children we only had two special outings every year, well guaranteed ones anyway. One was with the Ex Service Men's Club that my father belonged to, funded and organised. It was by train to Barry Island. The other was the annual January trip to the New Theatre in Cardiff to see the pantomime. We always went by train. Usually the Williams family who lived in Grove Terrace joined us for company. As we waited for the train to come in, our chattering and laughter could be heard from the surrounding streets. The excitement we felt in the weeks leading up to these outings was almost unbearable.

The queue to go into the theatre was always huge. Our seats were always high up in the back circle; the cheapest seats. Looking down on the stage and hearing the orchestra tune up, the magic would begin. Mesmerised as we were, we would almost forget to eat the small bag of dolly mixtures or packets of chocolate drops that we were allowed. The sequined costumes of the dancers had my sisters and I spellbound. 'Whooo. Ahhhh,' we gasped to one another. I wanted to cry when the pantomime ended and the audience stood. As the cast came out in turn and bowed in their magnificent costumes we clapped until our hands stung. We had to wait a whole year for the joy of this day to come around again. Whilst walking back to the railway station we would discuss our favourite parts of the show. It was always an afternoon matinee, so we would be home before dark.

The Barry Island trip was also thrilling. Clutching plastic buckets and spades we made our way down to the station, directly in front of our house. My mother would carry a bag packed with our lunch – paste or cheese sandwiches, some tinned salmon ones for my father, cake, and bananas. My father would be carrying the towels and swimming costumes. Although none of us could swim, we loved to jump over the shallow waves. On the train my sister Joyce and I would sit together and Ray and Linda would sit together besides my mother. We wore cool cotton dresses and our hair in plaits. Ray and Linda did not have long hair but my mother always tied theirs back from their eyes. When the train passed Caerphilly and entered the tunnel we would all shriek until the lights came on. It was so very noisy, some of the windows were left open and very little ones cried at the experience. When the train emerged out of the tunnel at Llanishen, a cheer would erupt.

When we finally got to the beach, my mother would always insist we settled on a spot near the first aid hut because it was next to the lost children's' office. Children who became lost would have their names announced on a loud speaker from this place. The sea walls were numbered and my mother would drum into us the importance of that number when you came out of the sea to find your way back to her . I so loved to see my mother laughing at my father's many attempts to open the rented deckchairs.

The fairground shows were yet another extravagance my mother couldn't really afford. However we were always allowed a customary three rides each. We longed to go on The Ghost

Train but that was forbidden; my mother thought it would cause nightmares. Our favourite was called The Cake Walk – an uncomplicated attraction with two wooden platforms that shook with vigour as they swayed as you attempted to walk across them. There were side hand bars to hold onto but we could barely grip them for laughing. We laughed at one another until our sides ached. After washing the sand off our feet with water from the tap near the penny arcade that we'd spent a little time in, it was time to head for the railway station again, tired out but oh so happy. Some dads and lads had 'kiss me quick' hats on. They added to the laughter of the day. On the way home we sang songs: 'Ten Green Bottles' and another favourite 'Show Me The Way To Go Home'. 'Our Linda is falling asleep,' Ray said and my mother lifted her onto her lap for the hour long journey home.

I loved the walks up to the mountains we called them Rambles. They were always to the same place and walked by the same route, to what we called the Water Quarry. A little spring of crystal clear water ran there. My mother would usually allow us to take one friend each with us. There would also be a couple of cousins and our neighbours' children. The group on these summer expeditions would usually consist of about fifteen of us. We took empty lemonade bottles or sauce bottles washed clean and any other bottles we could get our hands on to fill with the lovely water. After drinking and refilling our bottles, we would sit around the spring, plaiting the bulrushes to make small whips and making buttercup chains to hang around our necks. These were days of blue summer skies, butterflies and foxgloves when the world hardly touched us. I remember one such occasion well because it was when my best friend June Thomas told me where babies came from. It was a lovely sunny day and we were just standing in the street chatting. 'They grow inside your mother's stomach,' she declared. I looked at her in sheer disbelief; I thought she had gone mad. 'It's true,' she said, 'because my aunt Clara told me.' I never asked my older sister about this, or my mother, for fear they would think I had gone mad. Just then my sister Joyce shouted to me, 'Come on, we're going to the Water Quarry.'

Once a year our family went wimberry picking on Cilfyndd Mountain. Up there you could look down over Pontypridd. Wimberries grew on low little clumps of moss like bushes and did not stay in season very long. My mother would make wonderful tarts from our gatherings, always placing a layer of thin apple slices at the bottom of the tart first so that the purple juice of the soft fruit would not soak through the pastry too much. She would jokingly say to us, 'Don't pick the sheep droppings by mistake now.' Giggling, we would keep our backs bent picking the fruit. 'Don't shake your containers or the fruit will bruise,' my mother warned us. It was a labour of love to feel the warm sun on your head and back, and hear the gentle bleating of the sheep. We would all sleep like logs when it had been wimberry picking day.

Rewinding

In the hush of night while others sleep
I drown life's realities.
To drift in another time so sweet
when life was unburdened.
There special joy was mine
going back to another time.
Keeping company with memories
in the hush of night when other sleep.
To wait and want for pleasures rare
anticipation bittersweet to bear.
I soak in the innocence of childhood
although sometimes it wasn't all good.
Filed away moments only I can see
locked in a heart that has no key.
In the hush of night while others sleep.

The Whitsun Parade

The children in our street loved the Whitsun Parade, or Whitsun Walk as we called it. This was a custom that took place on the seventh Sunday after Easter every year. This special day was to celebrate the churches and chapels being built. Elders of the chapel, members, and children of the congregation all took part . Our family belonged to the Congregational Chapel, which is now called the United Reform Church. We were accompanied by St Peters Church and the

Salvation Army, which had a small band that would accompany the hymn singing. All would congregate outside their place of worship then join in one long parade. Each place of worship had its own banner proudly held by some of the older teenage boys. Children a little younger would proudly hold the gold silk cords attached to them.

Everyone wore their best clothes for the parade. There was much excitement in our house as sometimes we had a new dress for this special day. My mother liked to dress us four younger girls all the same. If it was not possible we certainly wore something very similar or the same colour. There was a time in the nineteen-forties when we wore straw bonnets adorned with artificial flowers and tied with ribbon. These bonnets caused our heads to itch and we scratched madly as if we had head lice. My mother scolded us, looking so upset; my sisters and I giggled but didn't complain too much because we so loved the pretty bonnets and there was so little my mother bought that wasn't practical and made to last. I can always remember the sun being warm upon our heads as we marched and sang hymns. Mothers and fathers stood in doorways and waved to us as we marched by. Never in my memory was there a wet walk out with umbrellas dripping with rain.

When we reached Senghenydd Square where the war memoriam is situated, we would stop and with heads bowed and a special hymn and prayer would be rendered. After the parade we returned to our respective church or chapel and a small Whitsun tea was served in the downstairs room where the children's Sunday School classes were held. Small tables and chairs were set out. The tea was very modest, just a couple of dainty sandwiches, tinned spam or salmon, plus a couple of iced fairy cakes. It would delight us nonetheless as if it was a huge banquet. The small plastic beaker of cordial served from a large white enamel jug brought delight too – it tasted heavenly after the singing and the walk.

Hanging on the wall of our Sunday School room was a large coloured print of Jesus. All around him were little children from different countries with different skin colours and different dress, all smiling. I loved the picture so much. I believe it still hangs there.

Dinner Time and Raincoats

My mother always served carrots, cabbage and peas straight from the saucepans they were cooked in. We did have some serving dishes, or tureens as my mother called them, but they were only used at Christmas when there was an excess of vegetables. The eleven thick heavy white plates that had been pre-warmed in the oven were laid out on the table – ten for the family and one for the meat. Warm food is more nourishing than cold,' she always preached.

Meals were served in two sittings because the house was small and we were many. Our table cloth was plastic-covered fabric secured under the corners with drawing pins, when the pattern wore off through constant wiping, my mother would renew it. It was only at Christmas and birthdays that the table in the living room was extended and a linen tablecloth laid on it. We were always told to eat all our carrots. 'You'll have better eyesight and even see in the dark,' my mother would declare. A downright lie. The simple truth was that she encouraged her brood to eat the vegetables with the most vitamins. Breakfast time we would invariably leave the crusts of the toast on our plates and my mother would preach, 'Eat your crusts up and you will have curly hair.' Little did she realise I already had enough curl in my hair and didn't wish it to be curlier. The fact was my mother couldn't stand waste of any kind. One day the gravy jug was spilled on the table and my mother shouted to my older sister to get something to salvage it. 'Anything you can put your hands on,' she said, 'before it runs onto the floor and soaks into the coconut matting.'

There was precious little in our house that was fine or delicate. Most things were bought because they were hardwearing or strong and durable. We had hard wooden chairs, which were placed on the small backyard once a week, scrubbed with a brush and left to dry in the sun. My sisters and I took turns to do this chore.

When there were wet days the recently purchased raincoats were brought out for my sister and I to wear. They were so stout and strong. Made of woven cotton with a rubberized backing, they could have stood up on their own. We hated wearing them. They grew heavier as the rain soaked into them. There were curved hoods on them with a huge button that fastened directly under the chin so that our necks were not visible. However rain would seep through the gap below the button and the wet rubber would chafe our chin, cheeks and neck. We complained in vain as my mother continually told us how much they cost and how lucky we were to have them. Bought long in length to last, it seemed we wore them for years.

Sunday School Anniversaries

Church and Chapel Anniversaries always caused much excitement as we usually had a new dress to wear and new ribbons for our plaited hair. The anniversary was a thanksgiving for the Sunday School. Most of the children in the Chapel took part. In the previous weeks to the Anniversary there would be many rehearsal evenings. Besides our individual pieces we had to learn new songs with three or four verses all joyful and lovely. There was always an afternoon and an evening service that proud parents would attend. A wooden step shaped stage was erected in front of the altar out of some scaffolding posts and wooden planks. This would be covered with green sheets of material to disguise its ugly crudeness. After the congregation had all arrived the children would file in from downstairs. The older taller children climbing high onto the back rows, the small younger ones were lower down at the front. All were encouraged to read or sing loudly as there were no microphones. The chapel pews were full even the upstairs as relatives of the children flocked to hear them sing or recite.

One year my sister Joyce and I sang a duet, neither of us had particularly good voices but we sang our hearts out and you could hear a pin drop, some children did bible readings' or read psalms . I remember singing solo Jesus wants me for a sunbeam, to shine for him each day. There was a chorus and the hymn seemed extra long to me. We loved the importance of being on the stage and the praise we received. There was always a murmur of approval but, of course, no clapping in God's house.

Family Bonds

Childhood seaside trips and winter pantomimes
Christmas gatherings with cine shows, fun times.
Sunday school sisters singing duets.
These passages of time I remember best.
Tea parties, cake, presents, winks and wine
births when pain and joy are shared
both with tear-filled eyes.
Family love encircling a young and shattered heart.
Secrets told to one another never to impart.
Siblings still bonded though an ocean far apart.
Family securely binds us with ties around our hearts.

The Parc Hall

On Saturday mornings the manager of the Parc Hall cinema had a one penny morning matinee. The line to the ticket box had a corrugated metal shelter over it so you were dry while queuing. Most of the children of the village would be waiting for opening time. They were always black and white films – some starred Roy Rogers or Gene Autry. I remember a character called Black Arrow who was always a scout for the main cowboy or the cavalry. We loved the Tarzan films that starred Johnny Weissmuller who had been an Olympic swimmer. Firm favourites were the shorts of The Three Stooges; everyone howled with laughter at their antics and hair styles. Laurel and Hardy the comedy duo also caused howls of laughter.

The cinema always smelled of orange peel as the floor was littered with it. My best friend's cousin was an usherette, and though she did her best to shush and quieten us, our excitement couldn't be suppressed. In the week there were evening shows; my mother took my sister, Joyce, and I twice a week. My older siblings were working now so she could afford these evenings out. My eldest sister, Margaret. would care for the two younger ones as my mother thought the three hour films too long for them.

The old Hollywood films were wonderful with none of the digital skills they have today. They had glamorous leading ladies like Rita Hayworth and Lana Turner and marvellous actresses like Bette Davies and Jane Wyman. How we adored the musicals with the great Fred Astaire and Gene Kelly. The actor Mario Lanza almost made me weep because his voice was so beautiful and he sang with such feeling. Heart warming, too, were the films that Shirley Temple starred in. There were thrillers that starred an actor called Boris Karloff but few of these films had the violence that exists in today's films. I usually left the cinema with a light and happy heart.

The Parc Hall later changed into a Bingo Hall , which made a new social life for many housewives. In my memory some of the happiest hours of my life were spent there.

The Transformation

A small secret concealed, safe, tied and neat
in the corner of my white lace handkerchief.
My first lipstick, forbidden, exciting and cheap
in a green metal case, used once a week.

At the Wednesday dance I twisted and jived.
My push-up lipstick I carefully applied.
Carmine lips in the mirror, gave a Lolita smile.
My teeth looked so white, my confidence was high.

A teenage temptress in cotton waffle dress
with gardenia-scented hair, my age you'd never guess.
For the rest of the week dark gymslip, plaited hair.
From my radio constant Beatles music filled the air.

In my pocket a treasure, my exciting treat.
I used it sparingly though it was cheap.
My very first lipstick, tied tiny and neat
made me a grown up, just once a week.

The Timepiece

When weary I climb into bed
my aching joints refuse to sleep.
In my head chapters of my life lie deep.
I turn back the pages to a Christmas past
in a cardboard box among my dolls, at last
my first wristwatch.

Silver and black, chromium-plated
it swamped my tiny wrist.
I gazed in awe and felt such bliss
and enchantment with the expanding strap.
I knew it couldn't really last.

I hardly ever took it off –
I wound it up both night and day
until the winder came away
and the magical ticking stopped.

The glass was cracked
and still I kept it long after that.
In a small cardboard box
my first wristwatch.

Christmastime

A month or so prior to Christmas my mother would make the Christmas pudding. I loved the smell of the candied peel, suet and dried fruit that was stirred into the mixture. My mother would always invite us to stir the pudding and make a wish while doing so. There would be some small silver three-penny piece coins wrapped in silver paper added. The mixture spooned into a china basin then covered in greaseproof paper and finally covered with a piece of white cotton, that was usually part of a worn out pillowcase. It was secured with a piece of white string. The pudding would be boiled then simmered for hours.

The Christmas tree we had was always a real one placed in a bucket that we would disguise with crepe paper. Tinsel and glass balls adorned it that had been carefully wrapped in tissue paper and preserved for many years. My father would stand on a chair and hang the tissue paper garlands across the ceiling. We would gaze up at them. They would sway with the draught from the old sash windows and the ill-fitting doors, and we would know the magic of Christmas was here. Our family was large and money was not always plentiful but Christmas was nonetheless exciting.

It seemed that on winter evenings in December we younger ones were bundled to bed extra early, calling 'goodnight. God bless' as we climbed the stairs. I later learned that my mother and elder sisters would sit around the living room table making dolls for us youngsters. My mother would buy the celluloid faces then hand sew the head, bodies, arms and legs on. They were stuffed with old laddered stockings that had been cut into strips. My mother knitted the loveliest dresses, bonnets and coats for them. Some were dressed in pink wool, others in white or blue. Narrow baby ribbon was threaded through the waist of their dresses and also attached to the bonnets. She also crotched little shoes for the shapeless fat feet. On Christmas morning my mothers and sisters patient hours were rewarded as we hugged, kissed and squeezed and then named our lovely dolls. There could never be any other dolls that were loved more than those handmade ones.

On Christmas Eve the excitement would be unbearable. After our baths we would sit around the table and write our notes to Father Christmas. The folded paper would be thrown up the chimney if a note didn't get drawn up and instead landed on the fire, we would hurriedly rewrite another. This was a ritual we performed every year amid shrieks and screams.

On Christmas morning we would find our presents set out on the chairs and settee of our three piece suite. We always had magic painting books that only required you to do a wash of water on them and the illustrations would turn pink or green. There were packets of wax crayons that snapped too easily, boxes that contained a Ludo board with Snakes and Ladders on the other side or another board game with a tiny dice and counters that were forever getting lost.

Silver paper balls covered in mesh cotton and stuffed with straw and attached to a yard of elastic with a finger loop gave hours of fun. In later years we would have chrome wrist watches, plastic shoulder bags, and real paint boxes.

Our Christmas stocking was one of my father's socks hung over the brass rod below the mantelpiece. When filled it would be placed with our other gifts. The stocking would contain small packets of dolly mixtures, liquorice pin wheels, sherbet fountains and packets of sweet cigarettes, which were thin rolls of hard icing sugar with pink-tipped ends to make them look more realistic. At the bottom of the stocking was always a tangerine wrapped in tissue paper, an apple, and traditionally a few brand new coins.

One year I had a wooden scooter my eldest brother had made for me. Oh how I loved it! I also had a baking set that consisted of a small wooden rolling pin and a tiny tin weighing scales that gave much delight, as did a small boxed sewing set with paper measuring tape and plastic thimble, small scissors and some cards of coloured cottons. I remember a Post Office box that contained a small note pad and tiny envelopes, some pretend gummed stamps and a rubber stamp that said Post Office. There were hours of fun to be had with such simple things. I often think how my mother must have saved so carefully to ensure we had them. I could never forget the joy of Christmases past because it's etched on my heart forever.

Fifties Female Friends

From the swirling-skirted sweetness
foxtrot-flavoured friendship of our youth
our lives never in sequence of a dance
like seeds we scattered and met perchance.

Branches occasionally touching on a tree
yet friendship has remained until maturity.
Comforting lunch conversations we share
trust and understanding permeating the air.

Images in time; photographs hold us fast.
As we peel away the years, memories flood back.
Confide, console, confess growing old –
elbows easy on a table, rested and relaxed.

The Divide and The Tears

Evan, my eldest brother, had worked in The Windsor Colliery. His wife, Molly, had been brought up by her grandparents who owned Caters, a small shop in Illan Road Abertridwr. Early on in their married life they decided to emigrate to Canada – Molly had been born there and her brother and sister still lived there. Evan had been more than happy to leave his job in the colliery but leaving our family was not so easy.

There had been other temporary departures in the family. Sylvia, my older sister, had joined the Land Army and my younger brother, Alan, had been called to do his National Service in the army and had been posted to Egypt. Alan was small in stature and his local friends had nicknamed him Titch. When he sent home photographs taken with his army friends my mother compared his size to theirs – he only looked about fifteen and she almost wept. My eldest sister, Margaret, remained at home long after our two brothers had left and helped my mother with us younger siblings.

When Evan and Molly made the brave, gigantic decision to move three thousand miles away, my mother wondered would she ever see him again. They made the journey to Liverpool where they boarded one of the Cunard Line ships, it would take six days to get to their destination. There were many tears from family and friends when they departed, though my parents disguised their worry and upset well.

Evan and Molly worked hard in Canada and it would be seven years before he returned home for a visit. When he walked into the living room of our old terraced house, the blacklead and Brasso fireplace had been replaced with a small cream coloured modern one. Of course, we had all grown and changed too. We all ran to him together and hugged him – the two youngest sisters, Ray and Linda, hugging his legs. He cried and cried, his tears dripping on our hair. I couldn't quite understand if he was smiling so much why was he crying? His mixed emotions of joy and sadness escaped me.

Several years later when Evan made another of his trips home, my brother Alan , who had now married and become a father, joined him in his return to Canada. My sisters Sylvia and Ray also decided to emigrate to Canada at separate times. They all adapted to Canada really well but it was Evan who returned for the most visits – I think his heart always remained in Wales. When he was home we called in on old friends and cousins and always walked the mountains and went to The Rec and looked down on the valley he still loved.

We were a family divided with half living in Wales and half in Canada. In the late nineteen-sixties my mother and father made the journey on a liner across the Atlantic, thrilled to be visiting their children in their homes. They had a wonderful time and I think it must have been one of the main highlights in my mother's life. Of course there is always the sad part of good-byes when hearts are divided between two countries.

Photographs

Photographs of years gone by transport us
to another time. Bring memories to our mind's
eye. Frayed and torn, the endure the years;
precious moments, hours and days replayed.
We are borne back ceaselessly into the past.

Step backwards in time into another era. Roll
back the years, sometimes blink away tears.
Memories dim, photographs revive. With these
precious images we remember, and are always
borne back ceaselessly into the past.

Photographs

Page i – Senghenydd Village.

Page ii – Linda wearing fur pixie hat made from neighbours
fur coat.

Page iii – Senghenydd class photo 1949.

Page iv – Me, Joyce, Ray, and Linda, wearing our Sunday
school dresses with Towser the dog.

Page v – Near the water quarry sister Margaret with us and
Towser the dog.

Page vi – Group photo taken by Evan on a visit home.

Back row left to right: Barbara Williams, Mary Jones, Julie
Williams, Linda, Glenys Ford, Pam Pedro, Ray.

Middle row: Afron Evans, Carol Lancaster, Fay Williams,
Valerie Williams, Jeanette Pring, Brian Eburgh.

Front row: Elverna Williams, Lesley Manship, Mair Evans,
Lynn Williams, Ann Evans.

Page vii – My mother, me, Joyce, Ray and Linda.

Page viii – On corner of The Rec. Me, with Evan home for
another holiday from Canada.

About the author...

Ethel Oates (nee James) was born in Senghenydd in 1938 and moved to Caerphilly in 1974 where she now lives with her husband. She has one daughter and three grandchildren. Ethel is a member of the writing group 'Caerphilly Scribes' who encouraged her to compile her childhood memories into this book.

Printed in Great Britain
by Amazon